Men-at-Arms • 474

The Chaco War 1932–35

South America's greatest modern conflict

A. de Quesada with P. Jowett • Illustrated by R. Bujeiro

Series editor Martin Windrow

First published in Great Britain in 2011 by Osprey Publishing,
Midland House, West Way, Botley, Oxford, OX2 0PH, UK
44-02 23rd St, Suite 219, Long Island City, NY 11101, USA
Email: info@ospreypublishing.com

Osprey Publishing is part of the Osprey Group.

A CIP catalog record for this book is available from the British Library.

Print ISBN: 978 1 84908 416 1
PDF ebook ISBN: 978 1 84908 417 8
ePub ebook ISBN: 978 1 84908 901 2

Editor: Martin Windrow
Page layout by Melissa Orrom Swan, Oxford
Index by Sandra Shotter
Typeset in Helvetica Neue and ITC New Baskerville
Originated by PDQ Media, Bungay, UK
Printed in China through World Print Ltd

12 13 14 15 16   12 11 10 9 8 7 6 5 4 3

The Woodland Trust
Osprey Publishing is supporting the Woodland Trust, the UK's leading
woodland conservation charity, by funding the dedication of trees.

www.ospreypublishing.com

Acknowledgments

The authors wish to thank the following individuals and institutions whose
assistance made this work possible: José Acosta; Gabino Ayala; Capt Félix
Zárate Monges, Paraguayan Air Force (Rtd); Capt Jaime E. Grau, Paraguayan
Navy (Rtd); LtCol Hector A. Grau, Paraguayan Army; 1st Lt Guillermo Fleitas,
Paraguayan Army; Rafael Mariotti; Gustavo Adolfo Tamaño, Colonel of Cavalry
VGM, Argentinian Army; Adrian J. English; Julio Luqui Lagleyze; Carlos Raul
Spinelli Larratea; Alberto Pino del Menck; Col Carlos Mendez Notari, Chilean
Army; René Chartrand; Cuartel de la Victoria, Paraguay; Colegio Militar del
Ejercito "Cnl Gualberto Villarroel," Bolivia; Colegio Militar de Aviación, Bolivia;
Museo Histórico Militar, Bolivia; Museo Historico Nacional Teniente General
German Busch Becerra, Bolivia; Academia Militar "Mcal Francisco Solano
López," Paraguay; El Instituto de Historia y Museo Militar, Paraguay; Unión
Paraguaya de Veteranos de la Guerra del Chaco; Circulo de Oficiales Retirados
de las Fuerzas Armadas de la Nacion, Paraguay; Museo Policial, Paraguay;
El Museo Historico de la Armada Paraguaya; and Escuela de Comando y
Estado Mayor del Ejercito "Mcal José Felix Estigarribia," Paraguay.

Artist's note

THE CHACO WAR 1932-35

INTRODUCTION

The Chaco War was Latin America's first "modern" conflict; it saw the use of the latest 20th-century military innovations, by armies that had learned some of the lessons – but that repeated some of the mistakes – of World War I. Motor vehicles, tanks, and aircraft were all employed, and some had an effect on the war; however, it was the infantry who bore the brunt of the harsh conditions, not only of combat but also of the extreme environment of the Gran Chaco region. Their experience of this war had an impact in their respective countries in the decades that followed. In a book of this size the scope for detail is obviously limited, but it is hoped that it will serve as a primer for those wishing to learn more about one of Latin America's bloodiest wars, as well as providing a general reference guide for those wanting quick answers on general topics.

* * *

The Gran Chaco is an area of about 250,000 square miles, though estimates differ. It stretches from roughly 17° to 33° South latitude, and between 65° and 60° West longitude – again, estimates differ. Located west of the Rio Paraguay and east of the Andes mountains, it is mostly a flat, alluvial sedimentary plain, divided by the national borders of Argentina in the south, Bolivia in the west and north, Brazil in the northeast, and Paraguay in the east. The climate is classed as sub-tropical, rising to about 40° C/100° F in July–August, but night frosts are not unknown in winter. The rainy season lasts from November to April, but rainfall varies greatly. It is particularly sparse on the central and western plains, where summer duststorms are frequent; the parched savannah grasslands alternate with expanses of cacti, almost impenetrable thorn scrub and low trees, with occasional palm groves around the few sources of water. The best-watered regions are along the Rio Paraguay in the east, and near Bolivia's Andean foothills in the west; here lush, almost jungle vegetation follows the watercourses.

Historically the Chaco has been divided into three main parts. The *Chaco Austral* or Southern Chaco, south of the Rio Bermejo, lies inside Argentinian territory, blending into the Pampas region at its southernmost end. The *Chaco Central*, lying between the Bermejo and the Rio Pilcomayo to the north, is also now in Argentinian territory. The *Chaco Boreal* or Northern Chaco lies north of the Pilcomayo, up to the Brazilian Pantanal; this is today mostly inside Paraguayan territory, but shares some of its area with Bolivia. (Inside Paraguay, people sometimes use the expression Central Chaco for the area roughly in the middle of the Chaco Boreal, where German Mennonite colonies are established.) The theater of war in 1932–35 was the Chaco Boreal, north of the Rio

The backbone of the Bolivian Army was provided by Altiplano Indians of the Andean highlands, who bore the brunt of the fighting and hardships during the war with Paraguay. They found the climate and terrain of the Gran Chaco extremely punishing. (AdeQ Historical Archives)

A sentry box made from the trunk of a "bottle tree," commonly found in the region. Paraguayans also call it *palo borracho*, or "drunken tree," since the trunk stores water in the extreme heat of the Gran Chaco. The image was taken at Gen Estigarribia's headquarters at Isla Po'í. (AdeQ Historical Archives)

OPPOSITE
Contemporary map showing the region of the Gran Chaco Boreal, with main routes, villages, and Bolivian and Paraguayan fortifications. (Map by Bob Gordon; AdeQ Historical Archives)

Pilcomayo, east of the Rio Parapiti and west of the Rio Paraguay (see map).

Politically, the Gran Chaco had been disputed territory since the wars of liberation from the Spanish Empire (1810–26). Officially, after the emergence of the new independent nations, areas of the Gran Chaco were supposed to form parts of Argentina, Bolivia and Paraguay, with a larger portion west of the Rio Paraguay belonging to Paraguay. Originally Argentina claimed territories only south of the Rio Bermejo, until Paraguay's defeat in the War of the Triple Alliance in 1870 established its current border with Argentina further north. Although the region was wild and sparsely populated, control of the Rio Paraguay running through it would give one of the two landlocked nations – Paraguay and Bolivia – access to the distant Atlantic Ocean, via its confluence with the Rio Paraná and eventually the Rio de la Plata, flowing to its estuary at Buenos Aires. This was especially important to Bolivia, which had lost its stretch of Pacific Ocean coast to Chile in the War of the Pacific (1879–83). In international arbitration, Bolivia argued that the region had been part of the original Spanish colonial province of Moxos and Chiquitos, to which Bolivia was heir.

Furthermore, the discovery of oil in the Andean foothills sparked speculation that the Chaco itself might be a rich source of petroleum. Foreign oil companies were involved in the exploration: companies mainly linked to Standard Oil backed Bolivia, while Shell Oil supported Paraguay. Standard was already producing oil from wells in the high hills of eastern Bolivia, around Villa Montes on the Rio Pilcomayo, and sought access to the Rio Paraguay for shipping it down to the Atlantic. However, Paraguay had lost almost half of its territory to Brazil and Argentina in the War of the Triple Alliance; with a far smaller population than Bolivia, it was not prepared to see what it perceived as its last chance for a viable economy fall victim to Bolivia's claim over potentially valuable territory.

Over decades, Bolivia began to force the natives out and plant settlements in the unexploited wilderness of the Gran Chaco. Although Paraguay claimed ownership of the region – where the small indigenous population of Guaraní-speaking tribes were related to Paraguay's own strong Guaraní heritage – it was slower to colonize the Chaco. However, before long both Paraguayan and Argentinian settlers were breeding cattle and exploiting *quebracho* woodlands in the south and east, and sugar cane was being planted within commercial reach of the Paraguayan capital, Asunción. This creeping mutual settlement encouraged both Bolivia and Paraguay to make military probes into the disputed territory, and, over decades, the two countries moved inexorably toward a clash that would determine the final ownership of the Chaco Boreal.

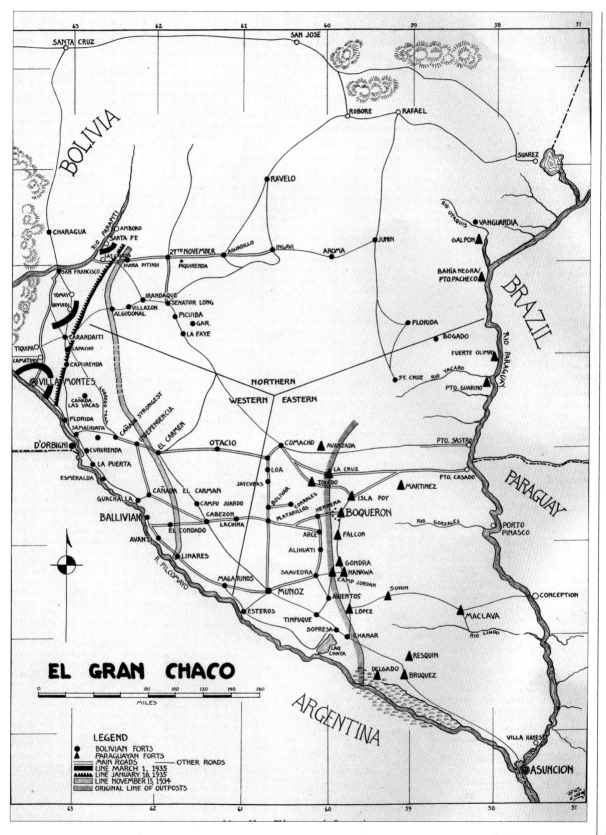

EL GRAN CHACO

MILES
0   80   100   120   140   160

LEGEND
● BOLIVIAN FORTS
▲ PARAGUAYAN FORTS
━━ MAIN ROADS ━━ OTHER ROADS
▬▬ LINE MARCH 1, 1935
▲▲▲ LINE JANUARY 18, 1935
▨▨▨ LINE NOVEMBER 15, 1934
▥▥▥ ORIGINAL LINE OF OUTPOSTS

5

The road to war

The first major clash between the Paraguayan and Bolivian armies occurred in December 1928, when a Paraguayan force attacked and captured the Bolivian advanced post of Vanguardia in the northern region of the Upper Paraguay river. The Bolivians retaliated by capturing Paraguayan military installations in the Pilcomayo sector in the south. Attempts at mobilization demonstrated the defects in the military organizations of both countries; neither was yet prepared for war, and consequently both were amenable to diplomatic intervention by neighbouring countries and by the League of Nations, leading to the return of an uneasy peace.

At the time of the Vanguardia incident the Paraguayan Army's attempts to mobilize seven reserve infantry regiments to join its five regular regiments had proved so chaotic that in 1930 a new establishment was adopted, of eight infantry and two cavalry regiments, an artillery group and an engineer battalion. In a new departure, regiments were named as well as numbered; the infantry battalions, which had previously been numbered sequentially throughout the Army, were now identified by Roman numerals within the new regiments. Additional equipment was also acquired, including 7,000 Belgian-made Mauser rifles, 200 additional Madsen light machine guns, and 24x 81mm Stokes-Brandt mortars.

Bolivian and Paraguayan military penetration of the Chaco continued, with both sides establishing lines of advanced posts. In mid-July 1932, Paraguayan forces attacked and captured the Bolivian Fort Mariscal Santa Cruz, provoking a Bolivian reaction that led to the capture of the Paraguayan posts of Toledo, Corrales and Boquerón in the Pilcomayo sector. Ultimatums were exchanged, and ignored; both sides mobilized; and within a month a state of full-scale (if undeclared) war existed between the two countries.

THE PARAGUAYAN FORCES

In 1931 an infantry division was formed at Puerto Casado, with the 2nd and 4th Infantry Regiments, the 2nd Cavalry Regiment and the 2nd Artillery Group. A second division was formed the following year from the 1st and 3rd Inf Regts, the new 3rd Cavalry Regt and the 1st Artillery Group. By now there was also an incomplete Engineer Battalion; the 5th Inf Regt continued to garrison the Upper Paraguay region, and the 1st Cav Regt formed a strategic reserve at Villa Hayes north of the capital, Asunción.

Paraguay had a population only one-third as large as that of Bolivia (about 880,000, versus 2,150,000 people). In June 1932, prior to mobilization, the Paraguayan Army totaled 4,026 men (355 combat officers, 146 surgeons and noncombatant officers, 200 cadets, 690 NCOs, and 2,653 soldiers). Both racially and culturally the Paraguayan Army was practically homogeneous, almost all of the soldiers being Spanish-Guaraní *mestizos*. On the outbreak of war a third under-strength infantry division was in the process of formation, but the projected creation of a cavalry division had not been realized. Paraguay's mobilized strength rose to some 24,000, with the two divisions in the major theater of operations under the command of Col (later Gen) José Félix Estigarribia. City buses were commandeered for transport, wedding rings were donated to buy rifles, and by 1935 Paraguay had widened conscription to include 17-year-olds and policemen; by the war's end approximately 150,000 Paraguayans would have served.

The order of battle of the Paraguayan Army at the start of the Chaco War was as follows:

Primera División de Infantería (HQ Isla Poy):
Regimiento de Infanteria 2 "Ytororo"
Regimiento de Infanteria 4 "Curupayty"
Regimiento de Caballería 2 "Coronel Toledo"
Grupo de Artillería 2 "Coronel Hermosa"
Batallón de Zapadores 1 "General Aquino"

Segunda División de Infantería (HQ Concepción):
Regimiento de Infanteria 1 "Dos de Mayo"
Regimiento de Infanteria 3 "Corrales"
Grupo de Artillería 1 "General Bruguez"

Tercera División de Infantería (HQ Bahía Negra):
Regimiento de Infanteria 5 "General Diaz"
Destacamento Olimpo (Naval Infantry & Artillery)

Projected:
Primera División de Caballería (HQ Puerto Pinasco):
Regimiento de Caballeria 1 "Valois Rivarola"
Regimiento de Caballeria 3 "Coronel Mongelos"
The organization of this formation was delayed by the outbreak of war; when fully mobilized it was to comprise Regimientos de Caballeria 1 and 7 "General de San Martin."

Paraguayan Navy
For the 50 years following the end of the occupation by Brazilian forces in 1876, the riverine navy remained very small. In response to tensions with Bolivia in the late 1920s it was upgraded, adding a small air arm in 1929 and acquiring new vessels in 1931. On the eve of war with Bolivia the Navy numbered approximately 68 officers and 600 enlisted men, including a detachment of Naval Infantry and a battery of Naval Artillery both assigned to the incomplete 3rd Infantry Division. The flotilla's role in the Chaco War was limited largely to the river transport of troops and supplies on the first leg of the journey into the Chaco, and to providing antiaircraft cover for the Army. Some naval officers also saw service as ground force commanders, and the handful of naval aircraft made a useful contribution.

This Paraguayan soldier wears the typical field uniform of a light olive-green shirt, trousers, and "Daisy Mae"-style sun hat, with a pair of light sandals. His field kit is a simple haversack and blanket roll, and a cow's-horn canteen, as home-made by Paraguayan peasants – see Plate B3. The Paraguayans' light and simple uniforms and equipment were better suited to the harsh conditions of the Gran Chaco than those of the Bolivians. Given the thick, thorny underbrush commonly encountered on those baking plains, this soldier's machete is as important to him as his Mauser rifle. (AdeQ Historical Archives)

A Paraguayan infantryman helping a wounded, injured or sick comrade. The Paraguayan soldiers were mostly Spanish-Guaraní *mestizos*; although largely Europeanized, they had managed to preserve many aspects of the Guaraní Indian culture, including its language. They proved adept at a more "guerrilla" style of fighting than Bolivia's more conventional army, and this would enable the Paraguayans to cut off, encircle, eliminate or neutralize many Bolivian units.
(AdeQ Historical Archives)

The *cañoneros* (gunboats) ARP *Humaitá* and *Paraguay* were built by SA Cantieri Navali Odero of Genoa, Italy, and brought to Paraguay in May 1931. During the Chaco War these little river warships assisted in the transport of troops and materiel up the Rio Paraguay and Rio Pilcomayo to the front. This wartime painting hangs in the Museo Historico de la Armada Paraguaya.
(Photo A.M. de Quesada)

Paraguayan Naval Flotilla, 1932–35:
Cañoneros *Humaitá, Paraguay, Tacuarí* (ex-*Adolfo Riquelme*)
Avisos de Guerra *Capitán Cabral* (ex-*Triunfo*), *Coronel Martínez* (ex-*Presidente Baéz*)
Balizadores *Capitán Figari, B* (ex-*Tesorito*)
Hospital Flotante *Cuyabá* (ex-*Aurora*)
Transportes *Almirante Brown, Castelli, Daymán, Desarrollo, Don Roberto, Holanda, Jorge 1°, Pollux* (later *Bahía Negra*), *Rivadavia* (later *Itápirú II*), *Rodolfo B., Parapití, San Francisco, Teniente Herreros, Tirador, Tucumán* (later *Itapê*)
Vapor *Posadas* (later *Teniente Pratt Gill*), Lancha *Clarita*

Captain José Alfredo Bozzano Baglietto, a naval architect and engineer, was the designer and director at the famous dockyards at Puerto Sanjonia (Asunción) and Humaitá. He was also instrumental in the procurement of the gunboats *Humaitá* and *Paraguay* prior to the war. As well as the transportation of troops to the front, Capt Bozzano supervised the manufacture of armaments, and the arsenal established in the Puerto Sanjonia dockyard saved Paraguay considerable sums of money. It manufactured some 25,000 mortar bombs and 7,500 aerial bombs, and more than 300,000 hand grenades, of a Paraguayan design known as *carumbe`i*, which proved to be more effective than the Belgian-manufactured SIP grenades used by the Bolivians. The arsenal also built and assembled the bodies of 2,308 trucks; Capt Bozzano's feats of ingenuity included the use of parts from old trams to make 23 mortars, and of 4,300 iron tubes salvaged from bed frames, stoves, and other items to make litters (stretchers) for the wounded. He also oversaw the employment of some 4,400 naval personnel as drivers, for the transportation of supplies and troops to the front and the evacuation of wounded to the rear. On 7 March 1933, Bozzano was appointed Director General of Aviation, in which post he continued his valued contribution to the war effort.

THE BOLIVIAN FORCES

In Bolivia, most of the soldiers (including 90 percent of the infantry) were indigenous Altiplano Indians and most officers were of Spanish ancestry, while the commander-in-chief, Gen Hans Kundt, was a German. In spite of the fact that the Bolivian Army had many more soldiers on paper, it never mobilized more than 60,000 men, and never more than two-thirds

Past and present: officers and crew of the ARP *Humaitá* during the war, and the foredeck of ARP *Paraguay* in 2010. Both ships were still serving with the Paraguayan Navy as floating barracks at the time of writing. (Museo Historico de la Armada Paraguaya/photo A.M. de Quesada)

of the army were on the Chaco at any one time – in contrast to Paraguay, which mobilized its entire army. In total, approximately 250,000 Bolivians would serve during the war.

Prior to mobilization the Bolivian Army numbered roughly 600 officers and 8,860 men. There were 13 regiments of infantry, five of cavalry, three of artillery, and four of sappers. These were organized into six skeleton divisions, of which only three were in the Chaco region: the 3rd (with approximately 1,000 men), headquartered at Roboré in the north; the 4th (1,200 men), centered on Muñoz in the south; and part of the 5th (600 men), based at Puerto Suárez on the Upper Paraguay. Total strength of the six nominal divisions was about 6,418 men.

The order of battle for the Bolivian Army at the start of the Chaco War was as follows:

1° Division (HQ Oruro):
Regimiento Sucre 2° de Infanteria
Regimiento Perez 3° de Infateria
Regimiento Campero 5° de Infanteria
Regimiento Ballivian 2° de Caballeria
Regimiento Aroma 3° de Caballeria
Regimiento Camacho 1° de Artilleria
Regimiento Pisagua 3° de Artlleria

2° Division (HQ La Paz):
Regimiento Azurduy 7° de Infanteria
Regimiento Avaroa 1° de Caballeria.
Regimiento Bolivar 2° de Artilleria.
Regimiento Pando 1° de Comunicaciones

3° Division (HQ Roboré):
Regimiento Colorados 1° de Infanteria
Regimiento Florida 12° de Infanteria
Regimiento Ingavi 4° de Caballeria
Regimiento Paucarpata 3° de Ingenieros
Bateria independiente de Artilleria

Hans Kundt (left – see also Plate F2) returned to Bolivia after World War I to serve as chief-of-staff and later as Minister of War, with the rank of general. As commander-in-chief he failed to fully exploit Bolivia's superiority in numbers, weaponry and aircraft, or to ensure effective logistics for the army in the Chaco. He also failed to keep track of Paraguayan troop movements, and employed futile frontal-assault tactics against well-defended positions (though he was not alone in that failing). Unit after unit of the Bolivian Army was surrounded and destroyed, and Kundt was relieved of command by President Salamanca after a significant defeat in the eastern Chaco in December 1933. (AdeQ Historical Archives)

Members of the Bolivian Presidential Guard drawn from Regimiento Colorados 1° de Infanteria preparing for a ceremony in the capital, La Paz, wearing Imperial German cuirassier helmets – see Plate E2. (AdeQ Historical Archives)

4° Division (HQ Fortin Muñoz)
Regimiento Loa 4° de Infanteria
Regimiento Campos 6° de Infanteria
Regimiento Ayacucho 8° de Infanteria
Regimiento Lanza 5° de Caballeria
Bateria independiente de Artilleria

5° Division (HQ Puerto Suarez):
Regimiento Warnes 9° de Infanteria
Regimiento Quijarro 13° de Infanteria
Bateria independiente de Artilleria

6° Division (HQ Riberalta):
Regimiento Riosinho 10° de Infanteria
Regimiento Bague 11° de Infanteria
Regimiento Padilla 1° de Zapadores

MILITARY OPERATIONS

For the sake of clarity, the war has been broken here into three phases. The first section of this chapter describes the tides of battle from the beginning of the conflict to the defeat of the Bolivian forces in the Eastern Chaco, and their retreat on Fort Ballivian in the west. The second phase covers the operations leading up to and including the fall of Fort Ballivian. The third and final phase follows the Paraguayan advance from Fort Ballivian to the outskirts of Villa Montes, where the Paraguayans threatened the Bolivian general headquarters and the rich oilfields within the Bolivian national border.

First phase, July 1932–December 1933

During the summer of 1932, Bolivia and Paraguay were parties to a Chaco Peace Conference in Washington, DC. On 8 July the conference was halted by news from Asunción that Fort Lopez had been attacked by a Bolivian detachment. The following week an isolated battle occurred at Fort Santa Cruz, approximately 70 miles west of Puerto Guarino on the Rio Paraguay. The Paraguayans besieged this fort with 2,000 troops well supported by artillery, but withdrew after several unsuccessful attacks.

Bolivia replied by concentrating two army corps totaling some 50,000 men in front of forts Corrales and Lopez (90 miles apart). This modernized army was a new departure for Latin America, being equipped with machine guns, aircraft, and even a few tanks. Bolivia also called up four more classes of reservists for the front. Against this powerful force Paraguay concentrated three corps, totaling 42,000 men, along the fortified outpost line.

On 29 July the Bolivians launched the first offensive of the war, with the ultimate aim of threatening Paraguay's vital supply ports at Puerto Casado and Concepción on the Rio Paraguay. In the north, the Bolivian I Corps attacked Fort Corrales, which had been occupied by the Paraguayans during the summer, while II Corps flung itself at Fort Lopez and toward Suhin on the road east of it. Corrales and Lopez fell on the first day. The following day the northern corps stormed Fort Toledo, and moved against the strategically important Fort Boquerón; by nightfall on 31 July the Bolivian flag was flying over its battered defenses. Meanwhile, the southern corps had been checked in its drive on Suhin by a strong Paraguayan line thrown across the Lopez-Suhin road.

Unseasonal rains then came to the aid of the hard-pressed Paraguayans, converting the Chaco into a steaming swamp that effectively halted the Bolivian offensive. This weather persisted for a month, during which little action took place. Paraguay took full advantage of this interlude to rush reinforcements to the threatened front and to complete its mobilization. At the same time, Gen Ayala replaced Maj Bray as Paraguayan chief-of-staff, and Col Estigarribia took command of the Paraguayan forces in the Boquerón sector.

The Bolivian high command planned to renew the bogged-down offensive on 11 September 1932, with Isla Poy (Isla Po'í) and Paraguayan general headquarters as their objective; but their plans failed to take account of a new adversary – José Félix Estigarribia. Learning of the Bolivian timetable for the offensive, Estigarribia anticipated it; on 9 September, he suddenly attacked Fort Boquerón. Three desperate assaults were made on this heavily fortified stronghold in as many days, but

Prior to the Chaco War the Bolivians, being basically an Andean army serving at higher altitude, wore a heavy cloth uniform of German appearance, usually of green-gray wool. Beginning in 1930, Bolivia placed a contract through the British conglomerate Vickers Armstrong to supply lighter khaki uniforms and equipment. Initially the Bolivians considered including steel helmets in the Vickers contract, but after the financial crash of 1929 the order was cut back, and helmets were one of the items removed from the list as unnecessary – in the environment of the Chaco they would anyway probably have been unusable. (AdeQ Historical Archives)

each one failed. On the fourth day, 15,000 Paraguayans again advanced to the assault, but after the first waves sustained heavy losses Estigarribia changed his tactics, to a system of penetration and eventual isolation. Within two weeks Boquerón had been retaken, and Estigarribia was given supreme command of the Paraguayan Army in reward for this victory.

With Paraguayan morale at a high pitch, Gen Estigarribia now launched a general offensive. On 1 October 1932 he attacked with his I, II, and III Corps in line from the right. III Corps, on the left flank, was ordered to make a fixing and holding attack around which the main effort would pivot. By 10 October, forts Corrales and Toledo had been retaken, but at Arce the Bolivian II Corps brought the Paraguayans to an abrupt halt. For four days the battle raged around this stubbornly defended fort; then Estigarribia succeeded in cutting the Platanillos road in the rear of Arce, and the Bolivians, facing isolation, withdrew to Alihuati, 10 miles south. However, the pursuit was so rapid and vigorous that they were unable to reorganize there, and Alihuati also fell to the energetic Estigarribia.

Further south, the progress of Paraguayan III Corps was much slower. Nanawa and Camp Jordan were taken, and a powerful attack was directed on Saavedra, but there Bolivian resistance again crystalized, and the desperate assaults by III Corps were beaten off. Not even the junction of the Paraguayan field forces in front of Saavedra, and subsequent united attacks, dislodged the stubborn defenders. The Bolivians held out, while the Paraguayans dug in. Despite this hold-up, Gen Estigarribia must have been well pleased with the results of his offensive; he had taken some 15 positions, defeated the Bolivians' II Corps, and separated it from their I Corps.

Bolivia's position worsened when the winter wet season put an end to all large-scale operations. On 13 December 1932, while the rains were at their height, the Bolivians did manage to retake Platanillos, but no further action took place until March 1933. During this enforced lull the Bolivian government took two steps: it organized a third army corps, and it engineered the return of the German Gen Hans Kundt as supreme commander of the armed forces. General Kundt, an officer with World War I experience, had trained the Bolivian Army from 1922 to 1930, but had then been forced to flee the country after a revolution.

A Bolivian patrol making its way through the thick underbrush of the Gran Chaco. The Bolivians were largely unprepared for, and in many cases unaware of, the extreme and waterless conditions that prevailed over much of the central plains. (AdeQ Historical Archives)

1933

In order to relieve the pressure on Saavedra, Gen Kundt ordered a counteroffensive in the Corrales sector for 1 March 1933. This operation, delivered over the same terrain as the July offensive, forced Estigarribia to withdraw troops from the defense of Camp Jordan to meet it, whereupon the Bolivian I Corps attacked and captured that weakened position. Their offensive further north failed, however, and movement once more ground to a standstill.

The first three offensives of the war – two Bolivian and one Paraguayan – had resulted in relatively insignificant gains. However, when Estigarribia launched his second offensive on 15 December 1933, its success, together with Bolivia's logistic difficulties, all but ended the war. Before the stunned Bolivians could recover from it, they had been driven right out of the Eastern Chaco.

Early in December, Gen Estigarribia concentrated a detachment at Fort Delgado close to the Rio Pilcomayo for the purpose of attacking the right flank of the Bolivian I Corps. On 15 December this detachment moved through the marshes south of the Bolivian Fort Chanar and deep into enemy territory; it struck suddenly at Fort Munoz, and then began to roll up the rear of the Bolivian Army. In the confusion that resulted from this bold maneuver the Bolivian 4th and 9th Infantry Divisions (half of I Corps), which were attacking Nanawa, suddenly found themselves cut off. Both of these divisions finally surrendered with a total loss of 10,000 killed, wounded and captured, and the severity of this defeat was compounded by the loss of division trains, artillery, supplies and ammunition.

Colonel Enrique Peñaranda Castillo, with a reserve force of 3,000 Bolivians, moved immediately southeastward from Fort Ballivian to save the remnants of I Corps. Arriving on the flank of the Paraguayan column near Munoz, he attacked, and during the ensuing battle the Bolivian II Corps and the remaining two divisions of I Corps made good

The undeveloped regions of the Gran Chaco had few motorable roads, and both armies had to revert to animal transport for moving much of their equipment and supplies. This pack mule is carrying the barrel of a disassembled Paraguayan light artillery piece up to the front. (AdeQ Historical Archives)

their retreat to Fort Ballivian. As a recognition for his part in the battle Col Peñaranda received his generalcy, and succeeded Kundt in command of the Bolivian Army. Thus ended the first phase of the Chaco War; by this stage Bolivia had lost some 30,000 men, and Paraguay about 15,000.

On 20 December 1933, Paraguay unwisely accepted an offer of an 18-day armistice for the purpose of peace negotiations. The Bolivian Army made good use of the time to complete its retreat and to reorganize around Fort Ballivian, where work on the defenses proceeded night and day. By the time Gen Estigarribia returned to the attack the Bolivians were so strongly entrenched that it required 11 months of fierce fighting, and the ablest maneuver of the war, to force them out of Ballivian.

Second phase, January–December 1934

During the early months of 1934 the Gran Chaco resounded to the tramp of the marching Paraguayan divisions, as 80,000 men were moved westward to resume the struggle. For the first time, Paraguay's soldiers were on undisputed Bolivian territory. To meet them, Gen Peñaranda had reorganized his defeated army, secured fresh replacements, and taken up strong positions around Ballivian. Fields of fire were cleared, machine guns carefully sited, and a system of barbed-wire entanglements thrown up. Communication trenches connected the front lines with the reserve and support trenches, and the Bolivian troops lived in well-constructed dugouts; on the whole, Peñaranda's works followed the most approved lines. This all gave an added sense of security, and the morale of the Bolivian soldiers took a turn for the better.

The Bolivian defenses extended from Linares northward, bending around El Condado and Canada El Carman, and thence through the outskirts of El Carmen, in front of Independencia and Canada Strongest (see map); Peñaranda thus enjoyed the benefits of interior lines. However, with the Rio

A Bolivian crew operating a Vickers machine gun from within a bunker fortified with tree trunks. (AdeQ Historical Archives)

Pilcomayo and the Argentine border at his back, he faced the danger that a Paraguayan breakthrough north of Ballivian might cut off thousands of his troops from the rest of the national territory.

General Estigarribia had followed the retreating Bolivians slowly. Hacking new roads through the wilderness and improving old ones, the three Paraguayan corps moved steadily westward. The I and II Corps advanced along the Platanillos-Cabezon road, and III Corps on the river road from Munoz to Linares. Supplies were shipped to the ports on the Rio Paraguay, where scheduled motor convoys picked them up and carried them some 200 miles westward, to feed the 40,000 Paraguayan troops closing in on Fort Ballivian. Estigarribia made certain that his supply system could sustain a major offensive before he hurled his divisions at the fortress. The Paraguayan corps reached their attack positions early in April 1934. The II Corps, on the right, occupied the front facing from Canada Strongest to El Carmen; I Corps stood between El Carmen and El Condado; and III Corps continued the front down through Linares to the river.

Apparently forgetting the lessons of Boquerón, on 25 April 1934 Estigarribia launched strong frontal attacks all along the line. These were repulsed with heavy losses; he then attempted an envelopment of the Bolivian left with the 2nd and 7th Divisions of his II Corps, only to be routed, with the loss of 5,000 men taken prisoner and some divisional supplies.

Having failed to pierce the Ballivian defenses by unimaginative Great War-style methods, Gen Estigarribia now came up with the most brilliant maneuver of the war. The Bolivians had shown no desire to leave their entrenchments around Ballivian and give battle in the open, and this led Estigarribia to believe that he did not need a force equal to the Bolivian strength in order to contain them. He decided to put Bolivia on the defensive in the Picuiba and Ingavi sectors of the Northern Chaco; most roads in this area, which were protected at intervals by permanently-manned forts, led to the valuable Bolivian oilfields of Santa Cruz Province. By ordering a Paraguayan reserve force under Col Franco to threaten Santa Cruz, Estigarribia intended to provoke the withdrawal of some enemy troops from Ballivian.

Accordingly, one Paraguayan infantry division with attached corps artillery moved north on the Comacho-Picuiba road early in August

A Paraguayan field hospital in the wilderness of the Gran Chaco. Note the wide variety of uniforms and headgear being worn. (AdeQ Historical Archives)

The entrance to the command and communications bunker of Bolivian LtCol Manuel Marzana within Fortín Boquerón, held by a garrison of 619 men during an epic battle in 1932. After the surrender of the position the colonel remained a prisoner of war until 1936, but he later resumed a successful military career. (Photo A.M. de Quesada)

1934. The advance was rapid; by the end of the month Col Franco had conquered the entire Picuiba sector, capturing La Faye, Picuiba, Senator Long, Irandaque, and "27 November" – all key forts in the area. Franco now sent his main body, numbering 12,000 men, down the Irandaque-Carandaiti road, while a smaller force advanced by the road from "27 November" toward the Rio Parapiti and San Francisco. The mission of both columns was to menace the main line of Bolivian communications running north from Villa Montes on the Pilcomayo to San Francisco on the Parapiti.

To meet this threat, Gen Peñaranda ordered his 7th Division from I Corps, and Col Rivas' cavalry division, all under the command of Col David Toro, to march north. The cavalry cut their way through jungle country (see map, "Lobedo Trail"), and arrived just in time to stop Franco's force at Carandaiti, where a fierce battle ensued for possession of the town. At this point Estigarribia ordered Franco to retreat slowly on Fort Senator Long. The Bolivians followed closely, satisfied that they had saved the oilfields from the enemy. By 14 November, Franco's coat-trailing had accomplished its purpose even better than Estigarribia had hoped: 12,000 Bolivians – instead of the 10,000 he had anticipated, and including Col Rivas' crack cavalry – were now all of 275 miles from Fort Ballivian. On that day, Estigarribia struck.

His orders for the operation called for a spearhead attack by his I Corps in the Canada El Carman sector, while II Corps on its right and III Corps on its left were to deliver assaults on their fronts to prevent Bolivian reinforcement of the center facing I Corps. Any advance by Paraguayan II or III Corps was to conform to the progress of I Corps. The attack jumped off on the afternoon of 14 November, and Fort El Carmen was the first position to fall. This part of the line was held by the 9th Reserve Division and 10th Regular Division of the Bolivian II Corps. The front-line regiments of the 10th Division were completely surprised, and the Paraguayan I Corps pushed on to division headquarters at Independencia, capturing the divisional staff at their desks. Before dawn on the 15th, the Bolivian 9th and 10th Divisions had been virtually annihilated, not one of their nine infantry regiments escaping intact. Here alone, the Bolivians lost 7,000 men, including 200 officers, the 10th Division staff, the divisional archives, and large quantities of supplies and ammunition, while Paraguayan losses were comparatively small. The Paraguayan II and III Corps also advanced in their sectors, driving back the Bolivian I Corps (less 7th Division) on the southern front, and their III Corps on the Bolivian left flank.

General Peñaranda expected Estigarribia to exploit his breakthrough at El Carmen by turning northward and attacking his III Corps, but Estigarribia had other plans. He ordered his I Corps to push southward straight through to the Rio Pilcomayo, meanwhile holding up the advance of his III Corps so as not to drive the Bolivian I Corps from the salient before the advance of his own I Corps cut their line of retreat. The Paraguayan I Corps continued its penetration; the Bolivian defense lacked depth, owing largely to the withdrawals for the northern front, and once the main line had been penetrated the Paraguayans advanced more or less at will. By nightfall on 15 November the advanced echelons of I Corps were within a few miles of Fort Ballivian, but withheld their fire to gain the advantage of surprise on the morrow.

At dawn on the 16th, Estigarribia's troops closed in on Guachalla and Ballivian, and by noon his I Corps had reached the Pilcomayo and those two forts had fallen. The Bolivians in the southern defenses, learning that the enemy was in their rear, now started a precipitous retreat for Villa Montes, but it was too late – the salient was closed. Thousands were caught in the pocket; some succeeded in cutting their way through the Paraguayan ring, others fled across the Argentine border, but for most of the men in this sector the war was over.

José Félix Estigarribia had led his fiery little army to another smashing victory. Fort Ballivian, the key to the Rio Pilcomayo, was his; in addition, his men had taken prisoner some 500 Bolivian officers including two divisional commanders, 16 regimental commanders, and 26 others of field grade. In all, some 8,000 Bolivians were on their way to the interior as prisoners of war, and 7,000 others lay dead. Finally, this victory brought some $3 million worth of captured war materials pouring into the Paraguayan stores. For this tremendous success, Paraquay had paid something fewer than 3,000 casualties.

To sum up: since the beginning of the war, Paraguay had conquered 34,750 square miles of territory, and taken 130 forts. For these first two phases of the war, various estimates place Bolivia's casualties at 45,000, Paraguay's at 20,000. At the end of the second phase Bolivia's field forces numbered scarcely 15,000, while those of little Paraguay totaled about 35,000.

At this point the League of Nations once more stepped into the bloody arena, with another peace proposal. Bolivia rejected this, on the grounds that it did not contain a clause submitting the entire territorial dispute to arbitration. The Paraguayans refused to consider it because its provisions would oblige them to evacuate Fort Ballivian – which was, of course, out of the question so soon after its triumphant capture. Moreover, Paraguay had already suffered one severe setback as a result of the December 1933 truce; Estigarribia was not going to make that mistake again.

On 27 November 1934, Bolivian generals, frustrated by the progress of the war, arrested President Daniel Salamanca while he was visiting their headquarters in Villa Montes – the 34th *coup d'etat* in the 107 years of Bolivia's national existence. After a very brief interregnum the vice-president, José Luis Tejada Sorzano, officially succeeded to the presidency.

Bolivian soldiers taking a break from the trenches to enjoy a meal inside a *fortin*. Scenes such as this became increasingly rare as the Bolivian supply lines were overstretched, and many Bolivian units were cut off by Paraguayan advances. (AdeQ Historical Archives)

A long-dead Bolivian soldier in Fort Boquerón. The failure of supply lines – and particularly of water supplies, in this arid climate – played a key role during the conflict. If cut off for long, many men were driven to the brink of madness by hunger and thirst, and would venture out into the wilderness, never to be seen again. There were thousands of non-combat casualties due to dehydration, mostly among Bolivian troops. (AdeQ Historical Archives)

Third phase, December 1934–June 1935

In the latter part of the war Paraguay became the *de facto* occupier of the Chaco Boreal. Bolivia retained only a small strip on the western edge of the jungle, about 150 miles long and varying from 30 to 60 miles in width. West of this territory lay the Bolivian highlands; to the north, the oilfields; to the south, the Rio Pilcomayo; and to the east, the Paraguayan Army. Bolivian general headquarters was now set up in the southern tip of this strip at Villa Montes, from which the main line of Gen Peñaranda's communications ran north to San Francisco on the Rio Parapiti.

Sizing up this situation, Estigarribia at once decided to try to cut the Villa Montes road, thereby separating the defenders of that stronghold from the remainder of the Bolivian Army located further north. Estigarribia now had some 30,000 troops in the field to Peñaranda's 15,000. To exploit this numerical superiority, he decided to push forward along the entire front, and thus prevent Peñaranda from opposing localized Paraguayan thrusts by concentrating rapidly in the threatened areas. In accordance with this decision, Paraguayan III Corps moved up river toward D'Orbigni, and I Corps on Canada Strongest, while II Corps was sent to the northern front to block the Bolivian advance in that sector. By 13 December 1934 the II Corps had once again captured forts Picuiba, Senator Long, Irandaque and "27 November," and had all but annihilated the Bolivian 7th Division by cutting off its water supply; some 4,000 Bolivians had died from thirst, 2,000 had been taken prisoner – such is war in the Chaco. The remnants of this division retreated on Carandaiti, hotly pursued by the Paraguayan II Corps.

Meanwhile, the detachment that Estigarribia had originally sent to the Picuiba sector under Col Franco had advanced to the Rio Parapiti, seized Santa Fé, and established a foothold in Santa Cruz Province. At the same time the Paraguayan III Corps, advancing slowly up the Pilcomayo, had captured forts La Puerta, Cururenda, Florida, and several minor positions. By 13 December this corps was only 30 miles from Villa Montes, but its advance was being stubbornly contested by the Bolivian II Corps. While his

Generals José Félix Estigarribia (left) and Enrique Peñaranda (right) seen together during the armistice meeting at Villa Montes, Bolivia, on 31 July 1935. Both men would subsequently become the presidents of their respective countries. (Courtesy Circulo de Oficiales Retirados de las Fuerzas Armadas de la Nacion, Paraguay)

III Corps was slowly fighting its way forward, Estigarribia's I Corps had smashed through Canada Strongest and then wheeled to the north to strike at Capiirenda; but almost in the shadow of this fort, Col Rivas' cavalry – Bolivia's elite formation – brought the enterprising I Corps to an abrupt halt.

After Gen Kundt's disastrous defeat in the Eastern Chaco in December 1933, Col Rivas had organized a cavalry division of five regiments numbering approximately 5,000 men, and threw it into the defensive sector of Ballivian. For five long months this division had surged around El Condado, and it had been largely through Rivas' efforts that many of Estigarribia's initial drives at Ballivian had failed. As mentioned above, when Estigarribia sent his diversionary force to open a northern front, Col Rivas' division was part of the Bolivian force ordered north to oppose the Paraguayans; Rivas rushed northward, cutting his way through the jungle, and arrived before Carandaiti just in time to save that important fort from the enemy. Now, in December 1934, Gen Peñaranda recalled Col Rivas to cover the withdrawal of the main Bolivian army.

Upon reaching the scene of the Bolivian retreat, Rivas threw his cavalry across the path of the Paraguayan I Corps at Canada Strongest, and contested every foot of ground, buying time for Peñaranda to reorganize his army at D'Orbigni. The Paraguayan I Corps was stopped dead in front of Capiirenda, and was held there until early in January 1935. During that month, Estigarribia turned both of Rivas' flanks and forced him to withdraw; this was Rivas' first defeat, but even so it was far from a rout. His well-disciplined regiments fell back on Villa Montes in an orderly retreat, and took up their positions in the defenses. The value of this highly mobile unit to Peñaranda can hardly be overestimated.

On 9 December 1934 the new Bolivian government, alarmed by the progress of Estigarribia's army, had ordered a general mobilization of the country's manpower. Women took over every duty they were capable of performing, and the number of replacements made available by this

As news spreads of the 1935 ceasefire, joyous Paraguayans run to catch a ride home on a transport. (AdeQ Historical Archives)

drastic mobilization is estimated at 125,000. Meanwhile, the government in La Paz had accepted the League of Nations peace pact; but Paraguay would not agree, and to its original list of objections it now added a new one. Since President Tejada had been installed by a military coup, Paraguay contended that his government was not constitutional, and that any settlement it made would not be binding on the Bolivian people. Thus ended another abortive peace effort, and the war continued.

By 15 February 1935 the Paraguayan Army had closed in on the Bolivian defenses. Their II Corps had turned the Bolivian flank at Carandaiti, and driven this force northward; one division was tasked with pursuing the Bolivians toward Boyuibi, while the remainder of the corps marched on Villa Montes. Contact was established with the Paraguayan I Corps en route, and this move cut the Villa Montes-San Francisco road, thereby separating the Bolivian forces. Meanwhile, the Paraguayan III Corps had captured Palo Marcado, and taken its place on the left flank of the army; both flanks of Estigarribia's army now rested on the Rio Pilcomayo, their right being protected by the Aguragüe hills.

Estigarribia now delivered a general assault on the encircled Villa Montes defenses. The attack continued for four days; by the end of the fourth day he had lost 4,500 men, several local positions had been improved, but nothing of any consequence had been accomplished, and the Bolivian defenses still held firm. Time passed; the Bolivians worked frantically on their positions, and waited for the final attack that they thought inevitable – but no attack came.

On the morning of 25 February 1935, Bolivian patrols reported that the Paraguayans had abandoned their lines around Villa Montes; the only traces that could be found of Estigarribia's army were unburied Paraguayan dead, empty machine-gun nests and abandoned trenches. Staff officers hurried to the front to confirm these reports, and found them to be true: Estigarribia had gone. The Bolivian communication net buzzed with frantic calls for intelligence.

Realizing that the situation at Villa Montes had become a stalemate, Estigarribia pulled back to reorganize. On 5 April, his II Corps renewed the pressure on the Bolivian rear by crossing the Parapiti, and probed along the Andean foothills; they penetrated as far as Charagua, which was captured on 15 April. The Bolivians were able to push the Paraguayans back, recapturing Mandeyapecuá (20 April) and Charagua (21 April), and thereby saving the vital oilfields. On the 23rd the Paraguayan 8th Infantry Division was surrounded, but managed to break out five days later. The Bolivian offensive continued until 16 May, when the Paraguayans counterattacked and pushed them back; Mandeyapecuá fell into Paraguayan hands once more on 22 May, thus canceling the gains from the short-lived Bolivian offensive.

Mennonite Colonies in the Chaco

In 1921 a law passed by the Paraguayan Congress in effect allowed German-speaking Mennonite settlers, fleeing persecution in Europe, to create a state within the state of Boquerón. The Mennonites acknowledged only Biblical authority and rejected all political claims on their obedience. In return for agreeing to colonize an area thought to be unproductive, these settlers were granted what was termed the *Privilegium* – exemption from military service and taxes, with freedom of religion and language, and the right to administer their own educational, medical and social organizations, law enforcement, and financial institutions. Major settlement began in 1926–27, when the Mennonites bought nearly 140,000 acres in the Chaco Boreal. The first wave of settlers were bitterly disappointed: the hard clay soil made agriculture difficult, there was no surface water, and no stone for building – just dust and thorns. An outbreak of typhoid killed many of the first colonists, but the survivors persisted; in time they found water, and created small cooperative agricultural communities, cattle ranches and dairy farms. Several of these banded together in 1932 to form the colony of Filadelfia, which became an administrative, commercial and financial center.

Just five years after their arrival, the Chaco War put the Mennonites in the middle of a conflict zone. They were treated as neutral by both sides, but were obliged to provide the Paraguayan Army with water, transport and food. The hospital in Filadelfia was appropriated by the Paraguayan Army, but provided care for the wounded of both sides. In turn, the military became a valuable market for Mennonite produce, and, of more lasting benefit, the Paraguayan government built a network of roads to allow military access to the Chaco. As the war passed through some of these Mennonite colonies the settlers themselves continued to demonstrate their humanity, while avoiding choosing sides. Their care extended to the dead; scattered throughout the Gran Chaco are small mass graves of Bolivian and Paraguayan soldiers, and while many have been reclaimed by nature those that are located on Mennonite farmlands are still cared for to this day.

During the early part of June 1935 the Bolivian 6th Infantry Division began an offensive from Raveló against a small Paraguayan garrison in Ingavi. The Paraguayans were able to send reinforcements quickly, and between 3 and 8 June a detachment under the command of LtCol José María Cazal was able to defeat the Bolivian 8th Division, capturing 23 officers and 200 enlisted men in what turned out to be the last major action of the war. In the following days the Paraguayans drove the survivors from the Bolivian 6th Division northward.

Ceasefire, truces, and aftermath

By this time both countries – economically exhausted, and suffering from increasing shortages of manpower – had become weary of the war. Paraguay controlled most of the Gran Chaco region by the time a ceasefire was negotiated for noon on 10 June 1935, although there was a senseless shoot-out between the armies in the last half-hour.

On 21 January 1936, the belligerents and six neutral countries (Argentina, Brazil, Chile, Peru, Uruguay, and the United States) finally signed a truce that renewed diplomatic relations between Bolivia and Paraguay, and agreed the release of all prisoners of war. Paraguay returned some 17,037 Bolivians, and approximately 2,498 Paraguayan prisoners of war were repatriated by Bolivia. Paraguay had captured about 23,000 soldiers (including 115 officers of field rank)

A symbolic statue of a wounded soldier of the Chaco War leaning upon the shoulder of a child, on the parade ground of Cuartel de la Victoria, the old soldiers' home located outside Asunción, Paraguay. (Photo A.M. de Quesada)

and 10,000 civilians – approximately 1 percent of the Bolivian population – and many of these chose not to be repatriated after the war. Another 10,000 Bolivian troops had deserted by crossing into Argentina, or had mutilated themselves to avoid fighting in the Chaco Boreal. In addition, Paraguay had captured about 2,500 machine guns, 30,000 rifles, 350 trucks, and 15 million rounds of small-arms ammunition.

Initially, the Paraguayan government in Asunción refused to allow any territorial settlement with the Bolivian government in La Paz, but cooler heads prevailed. The settlement was recognized in a 1938 truce, signed in Buenos Aires, Argentina, by which Paraguay was awarded three-quarters of the Chaco Boreal – 20,000 square miles. About two Paraguayans and three Bolivians had thus died for every square mile.[1] Bolivia got the remaining territory. Years later it was found that there were no oil resources in Paraguay's region of the Chaco Boreal, while the territories retained by Bolivia were, in fact, rich in natural gas and petroleum; at the present time these are Bolivia's largest exports and sources of wealth.

Bolivia's stunning military defeat during the Chaco War led to a mass political movement known as the Generación del Chaco, which shook the traditional order of society. Although President Tejada had brought the war to an end, extreme popular discontent led to a combined military-civilian insurrection that proclaimed Col David Toro as president. His government declared socialist principles, associating itself with revolutionary sentiments. It canceled Standard Oil's Bolivian exploitation rights due to concerns over the company's role in encouraging the Chaco War; and it instituted a Department of Labor, accepting some responsibility for the condition of the working poor for the first time in Bolivian history.

In July 1937 another coup placed Col Germàn Busch in power. Busch had been one of Bolivia's genuine heroes in the Chaco War; his presidency was well accepted by the population, but it soon floundered. In 1939 Busch supposedly committed suicide, and Gen Carlos Quintanilla assumed power. The after-effects of the Chaco War continued to be significant in Bolivian politics, as epitomized by the revolution led by the Movimiento Nacionalista Revolucionario (MNR) in 1952.

A final treaty clearly marking the boundaries between the two countries was not signed until 28 April 2009. The following year, on 12 June 2010, the 75th anniversary of the end of the war was marked by a meeting between Bolivian Defense Minister Rubén Saavedra and his Paraguayan counterpart, Luis Bareiro Spaini, in the frontier town of Villa Montes, Bolivia, in a public ceremony of reconciliation.

---

[1] The various sources are vague and contradictory over the total deaths during the Chaco War; the figure of 100,000 has been widely repeated, but the distinction between combat deaths, deaths from disease, and total casualties is often imprecise. One source gives Bolivian deaths in the field as 52,397 and deaths in captivity as 4,264, thus 56,661 in all, and Paraguayan deaths as about 36,000. If this is anywhere near the truth, giving some 92,660 deaths combined, then total casualties for both sides – by the conventional killed/wounded ratio of 3:1 – must have been in the region of 280,000.

Survivors

The Paraguayan veterans of the Chaco War formed the Asociación Nacional de Ex Combatientes in 1935. This body became a strong political entity that fought for pensions, relief, and other social benefits on behalf of the veterans. It was instrumental in persuading the government to provide a soldiers' home for veterans who were severely disabled or otherwise unable to care for themselves. This institution was officially inaugurated on 29 September 1945 under the name of Cuartel de Inválidos, but was later renamed Cuartel de la Victoria, in homage to the victory won by the sacrifices of Paraguayan soldiers. The facility is administered by the Paraguayan Army and the Ministry of National Defense, and each veteran receives a modest monthly pension in addition to medical care at government expense. The numbers of living Paraguayan veterans of the Chaco War are naturally in rapid decline; official sources state that 3,222 were still alive nationwide in 2008, and this had fallen to 2,614 in 2009. At the Cuartel de la Victoria there were 56 veterans in 2005, 45 in 2006, but only 8 by 2010.

The Bolivians formed their own Federación de Excombatientes de la Guerra del Chaco after the war. To mark the 75th anniversary of the ceasefire, in 2010 the Bolivian cabinet decreed the payment of a one-off bonus to surviving veterans, and a 5 percent increase in their lifetime pension; this increase would benefit about 655 veterans, 72 disabled veterans, and 6,205 widows of deceased veterans. The numbers of surviving Bolivian veterans are comparable to those in Paraguay; roughly 5,000 were alive in 2004, and just under 3,000 in 2010.

Salustiano Medina (left) served as a *soldado* for Paraguay, while Absalón Rivera Blacut (right) was a Bolivian *cabo*, corporal. By 2010, 75 years after the end of the conflict, the average age for a veteran of the Chaco War was over 95. (Photo A.M. de Quesada/photo AdeQ Historical Archives)

WEAPONS

Infantry

Pistols in use during the Chaco War included, on the Bolivian side, the Commercial Model 1906 Luger semi-automatic, some of which had been delivered in 1912, and the "broomhandle" Mauser C96, both from Germany. Another type in service with the Bolivians was the Browning M1911 semi-automatic, while the Belgian FN-Browning M1903 was a main type in Paraguayan service; they bought 304 in 1927, and may have acquired smaller batches before the war broke out.

Bolivia used a large number of Czechoslovakian-made VZ-24 7.62mm short rifles, importing about 39,000 in the late 1920s and a further 45,000 in 1933. A shortfall in the number of VZ-24s delivered was made up by a batch of German M1933 "Standard Model" short rifles. Belgian FN M1930 short rifles were also used in some numbers, as were Argentinian M1891 Mausers and the Bolivian M1908, all in 7.62mm caliber. Paraguayan Mauser-pattern rifles included the 7.62mm Belgian FN M1930,

The Ford Model AA truck was the most common Paraguayan vehicle for transportation of troops and supplies into the heart of the Gran Chaco. Other exhibits visible here in a regimental museum at Asunción are Vickers and Maxim machine guns, with a Schneider MPC 75mm mountain gun. (Photo A.M. de Quesada)

Paraguayan troops at a supply depot, with a 7.65mm Madsen M1926 light machine gun; Paraguay had bought nearly 400 of these before the outbreak of the Chaco War, and others were acquired during the conflict. One of the most widely sold LMGs in the world, the Danish Madsen was made in a dozen different calibers and supplied to 34 countries. Both the M1925 purchased by Bolivia and the M1926 supplied to Paraguay were chambered for 7.65x53 Mauser ammunition, so captures could be used readily – as was true of the 7.62mm Mauser bolt-action rifles and ammunition used by both sides. (AdeQ Historical Archives)

the Spanish M1927 and the German M1907. This commonality of basic pattern and caliber meant that any captured rifles and ammunition could immediately be used against their former owners. Non-7.62mm rifles in service with the Paraguayans included the Mauser Modello Chileno in 7mm, and some ex-British Lee Metfords in 7.7mm – the latter being leftovers from a hasty arms deal done by the Liberal movement during the revolution of 1904.

A surprisingly large number of sub-machine guns were used by the Bolivians during the war; the Paraguayans captured 935 of these on the battlefield, and put them to good use. Bolivia had purchased quantities of several models available in the early 1930s, including the Bergmann MP28, the Steyr Solothurn S1-100 and the Vollmer VMP30, all in 9mm caliber. (The Bergmann and Steyr looked very similar, and because of this other Bergmann and Erma models are sometimes quoted as being in service with the Bolivians.) In addition, some Finnish sources say that small numbers of the Suomi M31 found their way to the Chaco War. Some sources also state that the Paraguayans had some US Thompson M1928 SMGs, but there is no photographic evidence of this, and it is doubtful if they bought any SMGs of their own to supplement their ex-Bolivian captures.

The two main models of light machine gun in service with the combatants were the Czechoslovakian ZB26/ZB30 used by the Bolivians, and the Danish Madsen acquired by both sides. The Bolivians also had a number of Vickers-Berthier LMGs; despite the fact that in 1933 they sent 346 of these back to the manufacturers, there were still enough of them in service during the war for the Paraguayans to sell 233 war-booty Vickers-Berthiers to the Spanish Republicans in 1936.

Paraguay had gradually built up its small inventory of machine guns during the first decades of the 20th century. Six Maxims were imported in 1906. A further dozen 7mm Maxims were purchased from Chile during 1922–24, but many of these were worn out by 1932; some of them were

(continued on page 33)

PARAGUAY, DRESS UNIFORMS
1: General José Felix Estigarribia
2: Captain, Grupo de Artilleria No 2 "General Roa"
3: Cadet, Escuela Militar

A

PARAGUAY, SERVICE & CAMPAIGN UNIFORMS
1: Lieutenant-colonel, Regto de Caballeria 1 "Valois Rivarola"
2: 2nd lieutenant, Regto de Infanteria 3 "Corrales"
3: Private, Regto de Infanteria 1 "Dos de Mayo"

PARAGUAY
1: Surgeon captain, Medical Corps
2: Nurse, Paraguayan Red Cross
3: Captain, Military Aviation Service

CRUZ ROJA PARAGUAYA

C

PARAGUAYAN NAVY
1: Seaman, ARP *Humaitá*, guard uniform
2: Lieutenant, Aero-Naval Service, service dress
3: Ensign, parade uniform

1

2

3

2a

D

BOLIVIA, DRESS & SERVICE UNIFORMS
1: Brigadier-general, General Staff, dress uniform
2: Trooper, Regto Avaroa 1° de Caballeria, service dress
3: Major, Medical Corps, service dress

E

BOLIVIA, FIELD & SERVICE UNIFORMS
1: Sergeant, Regto Florida 12° de Infanteria
2: Major-General Hans Kundt
3: Second lieutenant, Regto Pisagua 3° de Artilleria

F

BOLIVIA, FIELD & SERVICE UNIFORMS
1: Sergeant, armored unit
2: Cadet, Colegio Militar
3: Captain, Air Corps

1

2

3

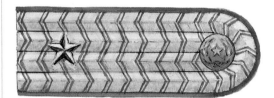

4

5

6

7

8

H

reported at the time to misfire after only a few rounds, and they would presumably have been discarded as soon as possible. Paraguay bought 32 Colt-Browning M1917 medium machine guns from the USA between 1927 and 1929. The Bolivians used the Vickers M1914 as their heavy machine gun, in various marks including the Type C, E and F, and Paraguay used captured Vickers in large numbers. After several Paraguayan victories the large number of machine guns captured meant that further direct imports were unnecessary.

The mortar was one weapon in which the Paraguayans initially had an advantage over the Bolivians, since they had 24 Stokes-Brandt 81mm tubes at the start of the war. Their usefulness in the terrain of the Chaco was not lost on the Bolivians, who bought some of their own during the war, as well as other mortars in 47mm and even 105mm. Paraguay captured 74 of these before 1935.

A prewar image of a Bolivian crew from Regimiento Sucre 2° de Infanteria with a Maxim machine gun, complete with ammunition-belt boxes and a range-finder.
(AdeQ Historical Archives)

Artillery

The Paraguayans had 49 pieces of artillery at the start of the war, the majority being 75mm mountain guns; they had seven German Krupp M07s, six British Vickers M87s, 24 French Schneider M27s, and four British Armstrongs. The other eight heavier pieces were 105mm Schneider M27s. Bolivia had bought most of its artillery from Vickers in the late 1920s to early 1930s; the order included 30x 65mm infantry guns, 47x 75mm mountain howitzers, and 18x 75mm field guns. Larger caliber pieces were 12x 105mm Mk C mountain howitzers and eight 105mm Mk B field guns.

Bolivia also had a number of light antiaircraft guns of two models in service in the Chaco at the outbreak of the war. The eight Semag 20mm guns could be used in both the ground and antiaircraft roles, but the 16 Oerlikon Mk 1 twin 20mm guns were used only against aircraft. Before 1936 Bolivia is recorded as purchasing significant numbers of twin 20mm Oerlikons of the L and K models – as many as 156 units, of which at least 56 were of the L type – and at least 40 were still operative with the Bolivian Air Force's AA defense units in 1940. Paraguay relied on captured AA guns, and took seven of Bolivia's Semags during the war. The Oerlikons that they also captured long remained in service, although they sold 14 of the Model L guns to the Spanish Republic in 1937.

Other known Bolivian weapons included six flamethrowers of unknown make, and a number of Oerlikon SSG36 antitank rifles.

Armored vehicles

Bolivia was the first Latin American country to acquire armored fighting vehicles and to deploy them in combat. Anticipating war with Paraguay, in 1926 Bolivia signed a large contract with Vickers Armstrong of Great Britain worth 3 million pounds sterling. At the insistence of Gen Hans Kundt, this initially included a dozen tanks, as well as rifles, machine guns, artillery, and aircraft. Although this contract was later reduced to less than

Paraguayan artillerymen manning a light field gun during their advances into the Bolivian-held interior of the Gran Chaco. (AdeQ Historical Archives)

1.25 million pounds due to the financial crisis of 1929, this still included three Vickers 6-ton Mk E tanks and two Carden-Lloyd Mk VIB tankettes.

The 6-tonners were of two different models, each with a crew of four men. Two were Type As, with twin side-by-side turrets each mounting a Vickers .303in water-cooled machine gun with an armored jacket. The third was a Type B, with a single turret armed with a short, low-velocity QFSA 47mm cannon and a coaxial Vickers MG; this had two turret crew, the commander and a gunner/loader. The two-man Carden-Lloyds were also armed with Vickers machine guns. These little tankettes, with mininmal armor protection, had not originally been designed as assault vehicles, rather as mobile platforms for emplacing machine guns on the battlefield, but improvements allowed them to act as mobile firing platforms – though since the gun was fixed to fire forwards, the practical field of fire was limited.

It has also been reported that the Renault FT17 was employed by Bolivia in the Chaco War, but this has not been proven. At least one demonstration example did arrive in La Paz in 1931, but it was never deployed to the Chaco. Towards the end of the conflict, Bolivia acquired from Italy slightly more than a dozen Ansaldo L3/35 tankettes, whose design was based on the Carden-Lloyd. It is rumored that the first units arrived in the Chaco in time to participate in the defense of Villa Montes in 1935.

A few German instructors had been providing services to the Bolivian Army as early as 1911, and in the Chaco War a Maj Wilhelm "Wim" Brandt

Paraguayan soldiers serving one of the seven Swiss 20mm Semag AA cannon that they captured from the Bolivians, and used against Bolivian fortifications and machine-gun nests as well as their designed targets. This weapon is also variously referred to as the M1921, M1923, or Oerlikon Model F. (AdeQ Historical Archives)

and Maj Achim R. von Kries commanded Bolivian AFVs. The rest of the crews were drawn from Bolivian volunteers who received eight weeks' training, and at least two of the mechanics were Chileans. Two other foreigners are recorded as having commanded armored vehicles: an American, Maj John Kenneth Lockhart, and the Austrian Capt Walter Kohn. Both died during the conflict – Lockhart during the battle of Kilometer 7 before Saavedra, and Kohn at Nanawa, which was the last occasion when the Carden-Lloyds were reported in action.

The combat history of the Bolivian armor is poorly documented, and such accounts as exist speak generically of "tanks," failing to distinguish between the 6-tonners and the tankettes. The handful of AFVs participated principally as mobile artillery in the infantry support role, but the Bolivians apparently undertook no specific training in such tactics. The armored unit may perhaps have entered combat for the first time in 1932 near Boquerón, where, according to Paraguayan sources, a "small Bolivian tank" (possibly a Carden-Lloyd) commanded by Lockhart tried to break the perimeter at Yujra to aid LtCol Marzana's hard-pressed garrison. On that occasion Lockhart was wounded by rifle fire, since he was operating the vehicle with the ports open due to the heat. Two AFVs commanded by Lockhart and Kohn saw action again during the battle of Kilometer 7 outside Saavedra, where Lockhart was killed after leaving his vehicle – due to the insupportable heat – to fight on foot.

One Vickers Type A was knocked out on 4 July 1933 by a direct hit from a Krupp 75mm; abandoned by its crew, it was blown up by Bolivian sappers to prevent it from being captured and used against them. The Paraguayans succeeded in capturing the other two Vickers tanks on 11 December 1933, in an ambush set up by the 7th Cavalry Regiment. While trying to break through Paraguayan lines the tanks were immobilized by Paraguayans cutting down *quebracho* trees ahead and behind them as they moved slowly along a narrow track through thick vegetation. After resisting with their machine guns for about 2 hours, the crews were forced to surrender by the heat inside the vehicles (more than 50° C/122° F).

Bolivian Army Vickers Mk E Type A twin-turret 6-ton tank, photographed after its capture by Paraguayan troops. The distinctive camouflage scheme is reconstructed on Plate G. (Courtesy Cuartel de la Victoria)

The same Type A tank as it appeared in 2010. For many years it was on display in a public square in Asunción; the turret from the single Bolivian Vickers Mk E Type B, mounting a short 47mm gun and a machine gun, was exhibited in the Paraguayan Armed Forces museum. Both were returned to Bolivia in 1994 as a goodwill gesture, and these relics are now both on display at the Colegio Militar del Ejercito "Cnl Gualberto Villarroel." (Courtesy Colegio Militar del Ejercito "Cnl. Gualberto Villarroel"/Col Gustavo Adolfo Tamaño)

THE AIR WAR

The Chaco War was the first international conflict in the Americas in which aircraft were used by both sides, both in combat and for transport, liaison and evacuation.

Bolivia began the war with a distinct advantage, its Cuerpo de Aviacion having 88 machines – quite a substantial number for the size of the country. The air corps had 16 fairly modern single-seat biplane fighters – 10x US Curtiss Hawk IIs, and 3 serviceable British Vickers Type 143 Bolivian Scouts (out of 6 delivered in 1930). Its 53 light bomber/reconnaissance biplanes included 20x Curtiss Ospreys, 9x Curtiss Falcons, 6x Dutch Fokker CVbs and 3x French Breguet 19s. Among 16 trainers on strength there were 6x Vickers Type 149 Vespa IIIs bought in 1928, which would also be used for low-level combat missions. Bolivia's transport fleet was quite modern, with (initially) two types of German Junkers low-wing, all-metal monoplanes formerly flown by the airline Lloyd Aéreo Boliviano (LAB): 8x F13s, and 3x W34s. The only non-German transport was a US Ford Trimotor, which had been donated by the richest man in Bolivia, but this was later destroyed in an accident.

The mainstays of Paraguay's much smaller Air Service were 15x French Potez 25 biplane light bombers (which would be reduced by attrition to a single aircraft by the end of the war). Before the war began Paraguay had bought only 7 single-seat fighters – French Wibault CL73 high-wing all-metal monoplanes – but these were joined in 1933 by 5x Fiat CR20bis biplanes. Three of the Wibaults were lost during the war, and the others were withdrawn from the front line in 1933. This left just the Fiats to perform escort and interception duties, and by 1935 only two of them were serviceable. Paraguay's transport fleet was also small, with only six aircraft of various lighter types, the largest being an Italian Breda 44. Paraguay had a small number of pilots and technicians still in service from the revolution of 1922 (a brief civil war in which both the government and the rebels had used aircraft for military purposes). Colonel Estigarribia could be considered an innovator in this field;

between July and August 1932 the Paraguayans built a landing strip at his advance base of Isla Poy, where they deployed practically all their small force of combat aircraft for reconnaissance purposes.

Combat operations

Bolivia's air operations were hampered by a lack of airfields close to the theater of combat, but despite this disavantage their Air Corps was able to conduct relatively effective attacks. Lieutenant-Colonel Bernardino Bilbao Rioja took command of the Air Corps in the Chaco, and initiated the air war in July 1932. He concentrated his assets at the primary base of Villa Montes, with an advanced base at Muñoz. At these forward airfields the Bolivians deployed the 3 Vickers Type 143 Bolivian Scouts, 3 of the Vickers Vespa two-seaters, and 3 Breguet 19 bombers. From the beginning, Bilbao ordered his aircrews to conduct aggressive patrols over the Chaco, and the Bolivians lost at least one Vickers Vespa to antiaircraft fire at the end of July.

Lieutenant-Colonel Bilbao visited the local Army commander, Col Peñaranda, and suggested that the best use of the Bolivian Air Corps was to bomb the main Paraguayan logistics base at Puerto Casado on the Rio Paraguay – a choke point through which every man, beast, liter of fuel and bullet entered the theater of operations. Later, in a violent confrontation with Col Peñaranda, Bilbao argued for the bombing of Asunción in order to demoralize the Paraguayans; from airstrips at Muñoz and Ballivián, the Bolivian machines would be able to reach the city. The Bolivian high command rejected LtCol Bilbao's demands; they believed, correctly, that bombing the enemy's capital city would cause international protests, and at this stage of the war they saw no necessity for such drastic steps (though they would later come to reconsider this). However, La Paz did authorize missions against Puerto Casado. These raids provoked a strong reaction on the part of the Argentine government, since many Argentines lived and worked in Puerto Casado, and ran the locomotives that linked it with the Chaco.

During the battle of Boquerón in September 1932 both sides flew numerous missions in support of their ground troops. Between 9 and 29 September, Paraguayan Potez 25s escorted by Wibault fighters carried out 12 bombing raids against Boquéron; the Paraguayans also used radio-equipped Potez 25s to direct artillery fire. According to Paraguayan sources, the first air-to-air confrontation occurred on 28 September, when a Paraguayan Potez 25 encountered a Bolivian Vickers Vespa. The Paraguayan pilot, Lt Emilio Rocoholl, was wounded, but was able to return to base. According to the Bolivians, however, the first aerial combat between belligerent nations on the American continent did not take place until 4 December 1932; the victor was a Bolivian pilot, Rafael Pabón, who downed a Paraguayan Potez. While he was seeking a second victim he was shot down by a Potez 25 (TOE No. 11), killing him and his gunner; the Paraguayans buried them with full military honors.

Given the modest size of the air arms, the cost in aircraft and pilots during the war was high on both sides, although most losses were due to operating accidents rather than enemy action. For example, two of Bolivia's Curtis Ospreys were lost in combat and four in accidents. Paraguay lost four aircraft, and four aircrew killed, in training accidents. During the war, Bolivia operated between 57 and 62 combat aircraft and

Personnel of the Paraguayan 2nd Aviation Regt, displaying two Madsen M1929 aircraft observer's machine guns. The majority of the combat aircraft that saw service over the Gran Chaco were two-seater biplanes, often with one fixed forward-firing gun and a flexible MG mounting in the observer's cockpit. (AdeQ Historical Archives)

22 transport and training types, and lost ten of them – six Curtiss Ospreys, two Curtiss Falcons, one Curtiss Hawk II, and one Junkers. Paraguay fielded 32 combat aircraft and 23 transports and trainers, and lost nine – four Potez 25s, two Wibault CL73s, two Fiat CR20bis, and one CANT seaplane. The main cause of the combat losses was ground fire, since air-to-air combat was relatively rare. However, when airmen came face to face aerial combats did occur, such as a rare clash between a Paraguayan Potez 25 and two Bolivian Breguet 19 bombers.

Some successful attacks were carried out against enemy airfields and supply dumps. The most successful Paraguayan attack of the war was against the landing strip and supply depot at Ballivián on 8 July 1934. Four Potez 25s, escorted by Fiat fighters, dropped 40 bombs on the airstrip, destroying at least four parked Curtiss aircraft and damaging others, as well as stores and other facilities. The Potez bombers also attacked and destroyed the main fuel dump at Ballivián, causing a severe shortage at a time when the Bolivian army in the Chaco was already suffering from fuel and supply shortages. During the battle of Carmne in November 1934, Bolivian aircraft covered the retreat of their cavalry by repeatedly attacking advancing Paraguayan units, and the Bolivian force's successful withdrawal was due in large part to the efforts of these aviators.

General air support

Although the combat units gained the most recognition, the unarmed transport and general-purpose aircraft of both sides made vital contributions. Both air forces employed a variety of types in a range of important roles at all stages of the war, including reconnaissance, transporting men and supplies, the evacuation of wounded, and even dropping blocks of ice to thirsty troops who could not reach fresh water.

In December 1932 the Bolivian airline LAB received three Junkers Ju52 trimotors, which were pressed into service by the Air Corps. Because of the logistical difficulties of supplying the army on the Chaco the transport fleet was vital to Bolivia's war effort, and during the war the Ju52s alone would carry more than 4,400 tons of cargo up to the front. Paraguay also pressed a wide variety of transport and general-purpose aircraft into service. At the end of 1932 two Travelair Model S-6000 six-passenger aircraft were purchased from the United States to serve as aerial ambulances. Both sides used aircraft for evacuating the sick and wounded from frontline airstrips to field hospitals in the rear, and over the course of the war the Bolivian Ju52s transported over 40,000 men to the rear. The carrying capacity of the Paraguayan Travelairs and Breda 44 was limited, but they generally flew a shorter distance to fully-equipped hospital ships anchored at the river ports of Puerto Casado and Concepción, and gravely wounded troops were transported to the Central Military Hospital in Asunción. These aerial ambulances flew constantly, and many Paraguayan soldiers were evacuated by air during the war.

This was also the first war in the Americas when political leaders were able to meet personally with their military commanders during operations in the huge, remote expanses of the combat theater. The Paraguayan President Eusebio Ayala used aircraft to meet with Gen Estigarribia and to visit the troops. Estigarribia was one of the senior officers who used light aircraft extensively for liaison with subordinate commanders throughout the region, and conducted his own reconnaissances over the front lines. The main Paraguayan liaison and courier type was the American Consolidated Model 21C (PT-11); Paraguay also bought at least one Curtiss Robin, two De Havilland DH60 Moths, a WACO Cabin, a CANT 26, and two light Junkers A50s for liaison and light support duties.

Naval air operations

Paraguay's Aero-Naval Service was created in 1929, with the help of the Italian aviator LtCol Ernesto Colombo. The service initially had a CANT 10 seaplane and an SIAI S59bis, followed in 1932 by two Macchi M18s. In addition the naval aviation service also shared two Morane-Saulnier MS35 and MS139 trainers, and a SAML A3, with the Army. Since all the troops and supplies for the Chaco campaigns were transported via the Río Paraguay, aerial control of the river took on considerable importance. The Navy based its small air component at Bahía Negra in the northern sector of the Chaco (see map – Puerto Pachego), in order to support the forces blocking any Bolivian advance down river. During the war the Paraguayan naval aviators flew 145 missions, including reconnaissance and ground-attack flights to keep the Bolivians under pressure around the upper reaches of the Río Paraguay. After dark on 22 December 1934, one of its Macchi M18s (R-5) attacked the Bolivian outposts of Vitriones and San Juan, dropping 400lb of bombs in the first night bombing raid ever carried out in the Western Hemisphere. (In commemoration of this accomplishment, 22 December is celebrated as Naval Aviation Day.)

The Bolivians also based a small aerial squadron in the northern Chaco, and attacked traffic on the Rio Paraguay on various occasions. Given Paraguay's dependence on the river as a line of communication and supply, the loss of a gunboat or large steamboat to air attack would have been a grave loss. To counter the Bolivian aerial threat the Paraguayan Navy used gunboats well equipped with AA weapons to escort troop and supply boats, as well as to provide AA defense at the principal bases of Concepción, Puerto Casado and Bahía Negra/Puerto Pachego. The gunboats saw some action, keeping Bolivian aircraft at bay in several encounters, and the gunboat *Tacuarí* is credited with destroying a

This Paraguayan six-seater Travelair Model S-6000-B served as an air ambulance and transport during the Chaco War. (Courtesy Cuartel de la Victoria)

Bolivian aircraft at Bahia Negra on 22 December 1932. Due to the efforts of the Navy, the Bolivians were able to inflict only minimal damage on Paraguayan river traffic.

Wartime procurement

For both sides the need to replace aircraft losses was complicated by arms embargoes imposed by the League of Nations and the US government. However, both sides showed ingenuity in evading these international controls.

Bolivia depended on Chilean support, since Chile had obtained licenses to assemble some Curtiss aircraft including the Falcon. As the Bolivians' Curtiss Ospreys were depleted by combat and accidents they wanted more of this faster type, and they were able to import a number of Chilean-built Falcons during the war. Chile quietly ignored the League of Nations embargo, and Bolivia also purchased examples of the Curtiss Hawk II and Seahawk through Chilean connections.

Bolivia had less success in acquiring four Curtiss BT-32 Condor bombers in 1934. This military variant of a large, multi-purpose twin-engined biplane could mount up to five .30cal MGs and had a bomb load of 1,680lb. Officially, the Bolivians wanted them for casualty evacuation, but given that they were ordered with military equipment including manually-operated gun turrets, machine guns, and bomb racks, this seems unlikely. It seems more probable that, in the light of Bolivian failures on the battlefield, La Paz wished to acquire aircraft capable of bombing Asunción. When the US government forbade the direct sale of the Condors they were bought via a newly created "front" company, the Tampa-New Orleans-Tampico (TNT) Airline. The four bombers made it as far as Peru before the US government and Paraguayan diplomats were alerted, and asked Peru to block their delivery.

In accordance with the League of Nations embargo, France blocked a Paraguayan order for ten Potez 50s, and the Netherlands blocked the delivery of five Fokker CVds. However, both Uruguay and Argentina were complicit in aiding the sale of armaments to the Paraguayans. Uruguay permitted aircraft arriving from Europe to be trans-loaded in its ports, and Paraguay bought a variety of training, transport, and liaison aircraft via Argentina.

FOREIGN INVOLVEMENT

Like other conflicts during the 1920s and 1930s, the Chaco War attracted a mixed group of foreign advisers, volunteers and mercenaries to fight on both sides. Both Paraguay and Bolivia had foreign volunteers in their ranks, with Argentinians fighting for the former and Chileans for the latter. About 300 Chilean ex-servicemen joined the Bolivian Army out of sheer financial necessity after their own army reduced its numbers drastically, leaving them out of work. The Argentinians in the Paraguayan Army served mainly in the 7th Cavalry Regt, which was named after one of their national heroes, Gen José de San Martin. Paraguay had a sizable White Russian émigré population, and about 60 fought during the war; they included two ex-generals, who were largely responsible for the design of some of the better Paraguayan fortifications in the Chaco.

Bolivia employed a number of German military experts (including the leader of the Nazi SA, Ernst Röhm). The most prominent was Hans Kundt, who as a major in 1911 had led the German military mission to Bolivia, consisting of 5 officers and 13 NCOs. During World War I, Kundt had returned to Germany and commanded a regiment on the Russian Front, rising to the rank of major-general by the end of the war. He returned to Bolivia, and was eventually appointed chief-of-staff of the Bolivian Army during 1921–26, and Minister of War in 1927. In 1930 Kundt was expelled from Bolivia because of political intrigue, but transferred his services to the Chilean Army as a staff instructor, and in

The sole surviving Paraguayan aircraft of the Chaco War is this restored Fleet Model 2. Five of these were purchased from Argentina in 1931 as trainers. (Photo A.M. de Quesada)

This Junkers F13 l/w floatplane, "BENI," served as a transport during the war. The Bolivian Air Corps pressed eight F13s of Lloyd Aéreo Boliviano into military service, starting in March 1928; this particular aircraft was powered by a 300hp BMW IV engine. Most Bolivian aircraft did not carry the Bolivian military roundels on the wings, but only rudder stripes in the national colors. At least four German pilots are known to have flown Bolivian tranport planes during the Chaco War. (Lloyd Aéreo Boliviano/AdeQ Historical Archives)

that role he planned some aspects of the Chilean/Argentinian border fighting over Patagonia in that year. Recalled to Bolivia on the eve of the Chaco War in 1932, Kundt was appointed commander-in-chief of the Bolivian Army. He was blamed for the serious Bolivian reverse in the eastern Chaco in December 1933; dismissed from the Army, he returned to Germany in 1934, and died in 1939.

In April 1925, Ernst Röhm resigned as head of the Nazi Party's *Sturmabteilung* (SA) due to a dispute with Adolf Hitler over the organization's future role, and in December 1928 he accepted the offer of a post as a military adviser to the Bolivian Army. The German government sponsored Röhm's appointment, and he was promoted to colonel in the German Reichswehr. With the Bolivian rank of captain, Röhm served on the faculty of the NCO academy, until Hitler asked him in January 1931 to return to Germany and the post of *Stabschef* of the SA. (It is said that Röhm based a new collar-patch insignia for that post – a wreathed six-pointed star – on those worn by the Bolivian General Staff.)

Altogether there were about 20 Germans in the Bolivian forces, serving mostly in the technical services including the armored unit. Recorded individuals included Maj Wilhelm Brandt (armor and infantry) and Maj Achim R. von Kries (armor); Maj Luis Ernst, Capt Werner Junck, Capt Walter Jästram and Capt Hermann Schroth (pilots, LAB Junkers Ju52 transports); an LAB air mechanic named Kastener; and Karl Heming, Walter Mass, Otto Berg and Karl Ackerman (all Intelligence). Prior to 1931 a Col Kraus and Maj Friedrich Muther had served at the Military Academy, but retired before the outbreak of war; there were also three NCOs, whose names are not recorded. In the closing chapter of the war a Czech military mission arrived to help the Bolivians, but was too late to have any influence.

One US citizen did serve with the Paraguayans – a wealthy New Yorker named Philip de Ronde. De Ronde, whose previous search for adventure had led him into the French Foreign Legion during the Great War, had a short spell as a volunteer in the Paraguayan 4th Cavalry Regiment. A number of foreign volunteer pilots flew with the Paraguayan Air Service, including a South African, a White Russian and two Uruguayans. During the first stages of the war the Air Force was actually under the command of an Argentinian, LtCol Alcides Almonicid. Bolivia also employed some foreign pilots, but on both sides the majority were their own nationals.

SELECT BIBLIOGRAPHY

Antezana, Luis, *Los Tanques en la Guerra del Chaco* (La Paz, Bolivia; Producciones CIMA Editores, 2010)

Brezzo, Liliana M., *El Paraguay a Comienzos del Siglo XX 1900–1932* (Asunción, Paraguay; El Lector, 2010)

Centinelas del Chaco, *Vision Grafica del Paraguay en Armas* (Asunción; Editorial Toledo, n.d.)

Chiavenato, Julio José, *La Guerra del Chaco Petroleo* (Asunción; AGR Servicios Gráficos SA, 1989)

Dalla-Corte Caballero, Gabriela, *La Guerra del Chaco: Ciudadanía, Estado y Nación en el siglo XX – La crónica fotográfica de Carlos de Sanctis* (Asunción; Ediciones y Arte SA, 2010)

English, Adrian J., *The Green Hell: A Concise History of the Chaco War between Bolivia and Paraguay, 1932–35* (Chalford, UK; Spellmount Limited, 2007)

Fernández Asturizaga, Augusto, & Julio Sanjinés Goytia (Cnl DIM – Ret), *Uniformes Militares Bolivianos, 1827–1988 y Condecoraciones Militares del Ejercito de Bolivia* (La Paz; Academia de Historia Militar Bolivia, 1991)

Fernández Estigarribia, Horacio, *Testimonios Fotográficos de Nuestra Historia* (Asunción; private publication, 2004)

Fundación Simón I. Patiño, *Chaco Trágico: Flora Doliente y Angustia de los Hombres* (La Paz; Artes Gráficas Sagitario, 2008)

Hagedorn, Dan, & Antonio L. Sapienza, *Aircraft of the Chaco War 1928–1935* (Atglen, PA; Schiffer Publishing, 1997)

Medina, Mariela Llanos Doria, *Guerra del Chaco 1933–1935* (Sucre, Bolivia; Casa de la Libertad, 2008)

Pastor Benitez, Justo, *Estigarribia: El Soldado del Chaco* (Buenos Aires, Argentina; Editorial Difusam, 1943)

Ratzlaff, Gerhard, *Cristianos Evangélicos en la Guerra del Chaco* (Asunción; private publication, 2008)

Sánchez Guzmán, Luis Fernando, *Boquerón 1932, Tomo 1 & 2* (La Paz; La Razón, 2009)

Seiferheld, Alfredo, *La Guerra del Chaco* (Asunción; SERVILIBRO, 2007)

Setaro, Ricardo M., *Secretos de Estado Mayor* (Buenos Aires; Coleccion Claridad, 1936)

Verón, Luis, *La Guerra del Chaco, 1932–1935* (Asunción; El Lector, 2010)

Vidaurre, Col Enrique, *Biblioteca del Ministerio de Defensa Nacional, Vol 4: El Material de Guerra en la Campaña del Chaco* (La Paz; Escuela Tipografica Salesiana, 1942)

PLATE COMMENTARIES

A: PARAGUAY, DRESS UNIFORMS

A1: General José Felix Estigarribia

General Estigarribia is depicted wearing the dark blue gala uniform, faced with scarlet and trimmed with gold, as prescribed for general officers. It shows a combination of 20th-century influences – Spanish, French, and German – but is basically a contemporary version of the style worn by general officers during the Latin American wars for independence in the early 19th century. The dress sword belt of silver brocade is interwoven with lines of red and blue. The three gold stars of his rank appear on the epaulets, epaulet loops, and cuffs; it was only after his death that Estigarribia was elevated to the rank of field marshal.

A2: Captain, Grupo de Artilleria No 2 "General Roa"

The officers' dress uniform prescribed in the 1930 regulations as "Uniforme No. 4, Etiqueta" shows strong Prussian influences. The national cockade in red, white and blue (from outside to center) is worn on the cap crown, above the officer's gilt wreathed star badge on the band. The three stars of this rank are displayed on the epaulets, the unit number on the collar, and the national colors in the epaulet loops, pouch belt, waist sash and sword knot. The facings and piping of the cap and the seven-button tunic are in the dark red of the artillery branch. Other branch colors were: general staff – black; cavalry – crimson; infantry –

scarlet; engineers – black on red; air service – light blue; medical – purple; military school – yellow and black.

A3: Cadet, Escuela Militar

The cadet's dress uniform is faced with black doeskin and piped yellow, with pointed blue buttoned loops, trimmed yellow, on the collar and cuff flaps. The epaulets are yellow, with open silver knots enclosing a wreathed castle emblem (**3a**). The cadets from the Escuela Militar formed the basis for the raising of Regimiento de Infanteria 6 "Boquerón" in 1932, and the unit received its baptism of fire on September 17 of that year.

B: PARAGUAY, SERVICE & CAMPAIGN UNIFORMS

B1: Lieutenant-colonel, Regimiento de Caballeria 1 "Valois Rivarola"

This field officer wears one of two distinct everyday uniforms seen in use by Paraguayan officers, in this case in khaki-brown with an open collar, worn over a khaki shirt and black necktie; the buttons are silver. His matching soft service cap is piped in cavalry crimson on the crown seam and upper edge of the band, and bears the same cockade and star badge as A2. On the tunic lapels he displays crimson pentagonal patches bearing the gold-embroidered cavalry branch badge of crossed lances over foliate branches. His shoulder straps, khaki with crimson piping, bear the rank insignia illustrated in detail as Plate H5. His "Sam Browne" belt, leggings and boots are in brown leather, and his sidearm is a 9mm Belgian FN-Browning M1903 semi-automatic pistol.

B2: Second lieutenant, Regimiento de Infanteria 3 "Corrales"

This campaign uniform was essentially the same for all ranks, with only the shoulder straps denoting grade. It is a German-style tunic with a stand-and-fall collar, a soft cap, and breeches, in a greenish-gray lightweight fabric, with subdued gray metal buttons. In the field most officers displayed minimal insignia, if any; instead, headgear, footwear, and personal sidearms were the distinctive signs of an officer or NCO. Usually the higher quality of the uniform also distinguished an officer from his men. In this case, some insignia are worn: the silver cord shoulder straps with a single rank star (see Plate H3), and the cockade, national star and scarlet infantry piping on the cap. The cap vizor and chin strap, belt, holster, leggings and boots are brown leather. He is armed with a .38cal six-shot Smith & Wesson Military & Police revolver (later known as the S&W Model 10, or, during World War II, the Victory Model).

At the time of the third Paraguayan offensive in 1934, LtCol Eduardo Torreani Viera commanded the 9th Division (General Reserve); this formation consisted of the 15th "Lomas Valentinas" and "Batallón 40" infantry regiments and the 1st Cavalry Regiment "Valois Rivarola." Compare this uniform with Plate B1. (Courtesy Circulo de Oficiales Retirados de las Fuerzas Armadas de la Nacion, Paraguay)

B3: Private, Regimiento de Infanteria 1 "Dos de Mayo"

This *soldado* in the trenches of a fortified position is wearing the basic olive-green light clothing worn by every fighting man sent to the Gran Chaco: a floppy-brimmed sun hat, a shirt with two breast pockets, and loose trousers – and note that this *mestizo* infantryman is bare-footed. His field equipment is limited to a blanket roll, a white canvas haversack on his right hip for rations and ammunition, and a large, traditional peasant water flask made from a cow's horn (the standard issue was a German-style aluminum canteen). He is carrying a Madsen M1926 light machine gun, and note the machete – an essential item in the Chaco, where much of the terrain was covered in thick, thorny underbrush.

C: PARAGUAY

C1: Surgeon captain, Medical Corps

As usual, this medical officer displays no insignia of rank, although his khaki tropical helmet (on the improvised tent peg behind him) bears the cockade and wreathed star. Over his faded olive-green shirt, with breeches, leggings and boots as B2, he wears a surgeon's cap, apron and black rubber gloves.

C2: Nurse, Paraguayan Red Cross

Many women answered the call to support their country in defense of the Gran Chaco, such as this female nurse from the Paraguayan Red Cross working at a field hospital. Her faded khaki uniform consists of a closed-collar shirt with breast pockets and concealed front buttons, and cavalry-style breeches and leather leggings. While the red Geneva Cross emblem was worn by noncombatants of both sides, photographs show that quite a few medical personnel wore personal weapons such as pistols and knives – probably due mainly to the need to defend themselves against wildlife encountered in the harsh conditions of the Chaco.

C3: Captain, Military Aviation Service

The Aviation Service was still a part of the Army at this date, and officers – like this injured pilot rescued from his crashed biplane – wore the same lightweight greenish-gray uniform. The branch of service is identified by the light blue collar patches with a gold winged star and chevron, and both branch and rank by the single light blue chevron of a company-grade officer, and the cloth discs backing the three stars of a captain, on his German-style silver cord shoulder straps. The pilot's ornate gilt qualification badge (see Plate D2a) is worn on his left breast above the pocket. His private-purchase brown leather flying coat lies across his legs.

D: PARAGUAYAN NAVY

The uniforms of the freshwater Paraguayan Navy differed little from those worn by the navies of Western Europe and the United States, with distinctive cap emblems, buttons, and dress swords.

D1: Seaman, ARP Humaitá, guard uniform

The traditional naval "jumper" and trousers are worn with a cap resembling that of the German Navy, a white undershirt with blue neck trim, a seaman's collar with single white tape trim, and a black neckerchief. The name of his vessel, the gunboat *Humaitá*, is lettered in gold on his black cap ribbon. For this duty the seaman wears laced white canvas leggings, a white leather belt with a brass plate bearing the national arms, and suspenders supporting the weight of two sets of triple ammunition pouches; when he goes on duty he will add white cotton gloves. His rifle is a Paraguayan M1927 Mauser; these were ordered from Spain, and made between 1927 and 1935 by Fabrica Nacional de Armas in Oviedo.

D2: Lieutenant, Aero-Naval Service, service dress

This pilot of the small naval air section wears white service uniform. The white-topped cap has a black band, black leather vizor and chin strap, and a gold-embroidered badge of the national star above a wreathed anchor. The double-breasted jacket has a falling collar and two rows of five gilt buttons; rank is indicated by the gold star and two braid stripes on the stiff white shoulder boards, and his qualification as a military pilot by the gilt badge (2a) worn on the left breast. The cuffed trousers are worn with low dress shoes made of white doeskin and black patent leather.

The appearance of the Paraguayan soldier in the Chaco War became a part of national lore and culture, and this figure in field kit even graced the front of a Paraguayan one-*guarani* banknote. (AdeQ Historical Archives)

D3: Ensign, parade uniform

For this duty the ensign has added to his everyday blue service uniform white cotton spatterdash gaiters worn under the trousers, white gloves, and his dress sword suspended from a belt worn under his six-button, double-breasted jacket. His cuff ranking shows the gold star above a single narrow braid.

E: BOLIVIA, DRESS & SERVICE UNIFORMS

Before the war the Bolivians showed very strong Prussian influences in their uniforms and insignia, as was typical of those Latin American countries that had hosted German and Chilean military missions. Much of the regalia – such as the officer's swords, belt plates, and *Pickelhauben* dress helmets – were in fact imported from Germany. (To this day cadets of the Bolivian military school still perform the goose-step, wearing Imperial German-style uniforms with *Pickelhauben* adorned with horsehair plumes, and regular soldiers wear World War II-style *Stahlhelm* parade helmets.)

E1: Brigadier-General, General Staff, dress uniform

The Prussian-style cap in stone-gray is piped scarlet at the crown seam and both edges of the band, and bears the national cockade in red, yellow and green (from outside to center). The stone-gray frock coat is piped scarlet down the front and at the top of the barrel cuffs, and the matching trousers have 3in scarlet stripes down the outside. The standing collar bears scarlet patches with the gold General

Two military chaplains of the Paraguayan Army. The priest on the left is wearing a makeshift habit of white cloth, possibly converted from a physician's lab coat, with purple trim on the cuffs. The chaplain on the right wears the traditional Roman Catholic priest's black habit, faced and piped in purple, with a pair of crosses on the collar. A gold braid above his cuff designates his rank as equivalent to a lieutenant, and series of gilt military buttons and black cloth-covered buttons line the front of the habit. (AdeQ Historical Archives)

Staff emblem of a wreathed six-point star. The complex epaulets on scarlet underlay have entwined gold-silver-gold cords (the silver interwoven with red chevrons), gilt crescents and silver bullion fringes. The silver brocade sword belt is interwoven with lines of the red, yellow and green national colors, and the gilt clasp displays the national arms in silver. On suspenders passing from under his coat the general carries a dress sword with a typical German-style "P"-shaped knucklebow.

E2: Trooper, Regimiento Avaroa 1° de Caballeria, service dress

The most striking feature of the uniform worn by this Indian soldier from the Antiplano highlands is a polished steel *Pickelhaube* helmet of the Imperial German cuirassier model, with a silver wreathed condor badge, and the bosses of the brass chin scales fixed through cockades in the national colors. His wool tunic, in a German field-gray shade, has a stand collar; patch breast pockets, with brass-buttoned scalloped flaps and box pleats; internal hip pockets with plain straight flaps; a fly concealing the front buttons; and turn-back barrel cuffs. The plain shoulder straps are piped in the apple-green branch color of the cavalry, and a brass regimental numeral "1" is fixed to scalloped collar patches of the same shade. He wears brown leggings and boots, but white leather waist and pouch belts, the former with a brass plate bearing the national arms in a raised circle. His weapon is the usual Mauser Gewehr 98 rifle. The other branch colors used by the Bolivian Army were: general staff – scarlet; infantry – red; artillery – black; engineers – reddish-violet; air corps – dark blue; quartermaster corps – light brown; and medical corps – pale grayish-violet.

E3: Major, Medical Corps, service dress

The officers' green-gray service uniform was basically similar but of superior material and tailoring. Hardly visible here is the piping on his stiffened cap, in the gray-violet of this branch. This also appears on the collar patches bearing a gold wreathed caduceus, and, for field-officer grades, as a center-stripe on the gray wool shoulder straps, which bear a single subdued six-point rank star. All leather items are brown.

F: BOLIVIA, FIELD & SERVICE UNIFORMS

Photos of Bolivian troops in the field show a variety of uniforms. They are mainly of khaki-brown cotton, ordered from 1930 onwards – alongside weapons and other equipment – through agents of the British Vickers group, but are occasionally of khaki wool, and sometimes mixed with headgear from the field-gray uniform.

F1: Sergeant, Regimiento Florida 12° de Infanteria

This NCO shows an example of such mixing of uniform items. His hat is from the gray-green wool uniform, with a brown leather vizor and the usual national cockade; photos show that all ranks often removed the wire stiffener from the cap crown when on campaign. The khaki wool tunic and trousers are from American surplus World War I stocks, with laced khaki cotton duck leggings over brown boots. His unit is identified by a brass "12" on his red infantry collar

The Bolivian commander-in-chief Gen Enrique Peñaranda with members of his staff. Note the varying shades of khaki-brown – compare with Plates F and G. (Courtesy Phillip Jowett)

patches, and his rank by three brass chevrons pinned to the shoulder straps. Shown in campaign order, he has a leather rifle belt with a circular brass clasp and two sets of triple pouches, and a German-style canteen in a brown wool cover hangs behind his right hip. His only other kit is a blanket roll, and a US World War I respirator haversack slung on his left hip as an all-purpose field bag. He is armed with the standard Mauser rifle.

F2: General Hans Kundt
The commander-in-chief of the Bolivian Army in 1932–33 is wearing a new khaki-brown uniform similar to those ordered under the Vickers contract, over a shirt and tie in a darker shade. His high-fronted cap is piped in the gold of general officers. His tunic bears on each lower lapel a single oak branch in gilt metal. His shoulder boards have a gold central stripe flanked by stripes in the scarlet of the General Staff, with the two gilt six-point stars of this rank centered.

F3: Second lieutenant, Regimiento Pisagua 3° de Artilleria
In the arid conditions of the Gran Chaco this junior officer has stripped down to his khaki shirt and darker olive-khaki breeches, but retains his "Sam Browne" belt as a clear sign of his rank amongst the men. His only insignia are the national cockade on his unstiffened cap, and the single subdued rank star on his shoulder straps. His sidearm is a P08 Luger pistol; the Mauser C96 "broomhandle" was also commonly used by the Bolivians.

G: BOLIVIA, FIELD & SERVICE UNIFORMS

G1: Sergeant, armored unit
Apart from the black padded-leather crash helmet of the tank crews, this NCO wears a simple outfit typical of Bolivian troops as the war in the Chaco ground on: a khaki shirt with his brass rank chevrons pinned to the shoulder

straps, matching trousers and American-style canvas leggings. In the background is one of the two Vickers Mk E Type A twin-turret tanks of this small unit; the camouflage scheme shows rounded patches of forest-green and chocolate-brown over a tan background, the divisions highlighted with black lines.

G2: Cadet, Colegio Militar
On 6 October 1933, Gen Kundt addressed the cadets of the military school: "Gentlemen cadets – those who wish to volunteer for the war in the Chaco, take three steps forward." The entire student body stepped three paces forward, and into Bolivian folklore; their unit at the front was nicknamed the Batallón Tres Pasos al Frente (roughly, "Three-steps Forward Batallion"). This cadet displays no rank, since he is not entitled to, but has fixed the gilt Military College emblem from his uniform collar – a wreathed castle tower – to his field-uniform cap, below the cockade moved up to the crown. He is armed with a Haenel MP28 sub-machine gun, a variant of the Bergmann MP18. On his officer's belt with its circular clasp he carries a leather triple pouch for its short magazines.

G3: Captain, Air Corps
The aviators of the Bolivian Air Corps usually maintained a smart appearance even when in a casual setting, as many of them were former civilian airline pilots. The khaki service uniform has an open-collar tunic with four brass front buttons, pleated patch breast pockets with scalloped flaps, and plain hip pockets with straight flaps. The only insignia displayed are the three subdued stars of this rank on the plain shoulder straps, and, on the lower lapels, a pair of brass winged-propeller Air Corps branch badges. He chooses to wear laced field boots rather than leggings.

H: REPRESENTATIVE RANK INSIGNIA
The rank system and insignia of Bolivia and Paraguay at the time of the Chaco War were largely based upon the Prussian style, first introduced to the Chilean Army by Gen Emil Körner in the latter part of the 19th century. Subsequent German and Chilean military missions later passed this system on to other Latin American countries. Prewar the only real difference between the officers' insignia of the two armies was the national colors of their respective countries incorporated into the cord braiding of officers' service and full dress shoulder straps: for Paraguay, red, white, and blue, and for Bolivia, red, yellow, and green. Enlisted rank insignia were a system of bars and chevrons. During this period the Bolivians and Paraguayans both adopted a new system of officers' rank distinctions for the shoulder straps of their field uniforms, but the Prussian-style corded shoulder straps were also used concurrently.

H1: Vice-first sergeant, Paraguayan Army, field dress
H2: Corporal, Bolivian Army, field dress
H3: Second lieutenant, Paraguayan Army, service dress
H4: Captain, Bolivian Army, field dress
H5: Lieutenant-colonel of cavalry, Paraguayan Army, service dress
H6: Major of artillery, Bolivian Army, khaki service dress
H7: Brigadier-general, Paraguayan Army, service dress
H8: General, Bolivian Army, khaki service dress

INDEX

References to illustrations are shown in bold. Plates are indicated with letters in **bold** followed by the commentary page numbers in brackets.